WHERE YOU START FROM

Where You Start From

LINDY BARBOUR

Poems

MARISCAT
PRESS 2015

ISBN 978 0 946588 78 7

Acknowledgements

'Small Town Christmas' won first prize in a competition run by the Sick Kids Friends Foundation, Edinburgh, and was published in the anthology, *The Gift of Words*; 'Small Town Summer Evening' was published in the Glasgow School of Art anthology, *Gliberagora*; and 'White Basin' can be found on the Poetry Society website.

And thanks to Liz Lochhead for starting me on my way.

—LB

Designed and typeset by Gerry Cambridge
in Miller
gerry.cambridge@btinternet.com

Printed by Glasgow Print + Design Centre
197 Bath Street, Glasgow, G2 4HU
www.GlasgowPDC.co.uk

Published by Mariscat Press
10 Bell Place, Edinburgh EH3 5HT
hamish.whyte@btinternet.com
www.mariscatpress.com

Contents

For James and Robin,
who were there

First, the Garden. November 1956

We opened the back gate in the high wall
and, entering from William Street, found you waiting.

You were pale and tired, resting in the November afternoon,
your grasses grown too long, adorned with fallen fruit.

Sunlight on your walls threw sharp
shadow branches of apple trees, plums, espaliered pears

and there were still some flowers; everywhere
white stars of feverfew, and by the path, a dark red rose.

A voice, my grandfather, with two years left to live, says
'You'll be chopping down that laurel, surely?'

My mother, who will tend you faithfully for forty three years more,
replies, 'That's not a laurel, it's a camellia.'

Every May she will cover it with a net curtain against the frost.

I stand beside the coal shed learning your scents;
the box hedge is pungent in the quiet air.

You are never so beautiful again
as in this first time of wilderness.

Where You Start From

Every day at teatime the brother and sister run
up two flights of tenement stairs past the landing
with the yappy dog and the castor oil plant in a tub.

The front door stands open and they rush through the hall
to the kitchen, where time rolls in spit balls on the Rayburn
and rises in the steam of the kettle;

where her job is to set the table with blue and white dishes
from the sideboard, and he, being younger, gets to sit
under the sewing machine and play with the treadle.

There is always jam in a dish with a fluted spoon, a battered
sugar shaker for the apple pie, a muslin cloth for the milk jug.
Nothing is ever too hot or too cold.

In the corner beside the wireless and the newspapers
and the chair reserved for the Airedale, is the spot
where one afternoon when the boy was three

his grandfather threw him up
into the condensation-laden air
up to the ceiling, shouting 'Sausages is the boys!'

Later, they remembered a picture in that corner
cut from a calendar and framed.
A green lane ran out of the kitchen, past a farm
and into imaginary woods.

Arrival

For James

I woke that morning knowing that it would be
the last time in our beds, the last time
listening to the coopers hammering
in the whisky bond across the street.
I was six and you were three.

After a journey of thirty miles, the train
slowed through three long cuttings
with sweating walls of black whinstone
and arrived in a small station. The platform
ran along the edge of a huge harbour.

We started up the hill into the new place
carrying our suitcases, past the Bell Rock Tavern
with its picture framed in a half moon—
the lighthouse standing on blue waves—
and a chip shop, which would later be demolished

after the husband, it was whispered,
hanged himself with the lavatory chain.
From there up a steep pavement, scored
in diagonal lines, and up the Broad Street Steps.
An iron handrail snaked to our new front door.

We spent the day sitting in corners, while they
unpacked and struggled to refit the lino
from the old kitchen, and at last
by teatime they set the table in the place
where it would stand for forty years.

There was fish and chips for tea, and before bed,
in a room with a gas mantle shaped like a whiskery cat,

a show of table fireworks with a small Vesuvius,
our four faces lit by sparklers and Roman Candles
in the dark new kitchen.

Small Town Christmas

Before the party we spend the afternoon
decorating the classroom
while the sky grows dark through the long windows
and the lights of the classroom
hang outside in the dark sky.

Frances Atkinson gets to help
because she's tall, pinning up the paper chains
we'd made earlier and the strings of milk bottle tops
washed but still smelling a bit
and a yellow and purple accordion-pleated bell.

We are clearing the desks to the side of the room
for the games and dancing,
when Petrena Connor gets up on a desk
and pulls up her skirt
to show her paper nylon petticoat.

The boys stop for a second
then go on running round with their arms out
being aeroplanes, till a fight breaks out.
Charles Anderson, a fat boy, who will become a policeman,
bends down to pick up a sausage roll, then screams for the teacher

because Frankie Rossiter has sneaked up behind him
and stuck a drawing pin in his bum.
'I wanted to see if it would burst Miss,' he says
and the teacher lets him away with it.
But only because it's Christmas.

I'm putting my Mum's mince pies on a plate
though nobody wants to eat them because they're home-made
when Jimmy Syme, who hates me, says, 'They're weird,'
and stamps on my foot.

But it was a good party

and afterwards we go back down the street,
past the Christmas tree outside the hairdresser's
and the blue and red bottles in the chemist's window.
It is a cold night, with frost on the ground,
and above the streetlights, the stars.

Eric and Ivor

Home was a street like a stone canyon
but when the holidays came
and they visited a garden suburb
the fairy-tale houses were radiant
with diamond-paned windows and porches
and white and green sunray gates.

She slapped down the street in her sandals
past crenellated low walls of brick,
gardens with crazy paving and hydrangeas
on pavements with grass borders
under a canopy of dark sycamores, and ran
into two boys called Eric and Ivor.

They asked her if she could keep a secret
and she agreed to go with them to look
at the maze at the bottom of their garden.
There, inside an unclipped double hedge
next to a creosoted fence, they crawled
into a tunnel, all three of them together.

Back up the street with knees and sandals
smudged with dust, what lingered afterwards
with the pungent smells of sweat and privet flowers
was a memory of hot green intensity,
an experience of close attention, the tingle
of rain in summer and the shapes of leaves.

River

It was a long walk up the road that June,
hot, and we walked in single file on the verge
of rough grass hedged with nettles and roses.
Dust flew from a Bluebird bus, a tractor.
At the bridge we climbed down to the river

and waded, legs cool and gleaming pale
through peaty water, feet tensed
against sharpness of shingle, slippery
boulders, stream-lined green with weed,
shifting and grinding on the river bed.

Stunned in the heat, and tranced
in a wavering net of light thrown
by leaf and water on the under arch of the bridge,
we spent the passing hours of the afternoon
in the constant, gentle voice of the river.

You can't get down there to the river now.
The road goes into a roundabout over the bridge.
Hedged in by light industry, the circle of traffic
frets and fumes, stopping and starting at the lights.
The river flows on beneath, unseen.

But every June I go back to the river
to find the dark pools under the trees,
echoing voices, reflections under the bridge,
the smell of summer—
hawthorn and nettles and river water.

Small Town Library

Out of the back gate and along William Street
past the rockers and their motorbikes outside the café.
The doors are open and it's warm inside and orderly,
the lino glows with polish and though you couldn't say
she's welcoming exactly, Jacqueline is at her desk as usual
putting the cards back into the ticket pockets.

One small room lined with books. The children's section
crammed with Bobbsey Twins and Malory Towers—
The Grey Lady looked down at them with eyes of stone!
The Aqualung Twins are in Mexico, diving for Aztec gold
and somewhere in the Alps the Chalet School girls switch
with bewildering ease from French to German.

Later, I will begin to teach myself French in the library
and contemplate careers like student nurse and air hostess
and when I'm ten, for urgent reasons I've forgotten,
will borrow a book about building wireless sets
and *War and Peace*. Jacqueline, while impressed,
is doubtful, but you can take the classics out on a children's ticket.

The adult section when it came, was something of a let-down,
lurid with Crime and Westerns, Mills and Boon.
The grown-up books seemed flimsy in their plastic jackets
beside the children's hard-bound blocks of rexine,
cream spotted on blue, brown and maroon. The doors
were closed long years ago, and Jacqueline and I are gone.

Spring Tide

The old harbour was small and three-cornered.
For many years the wreck of a fishing boat
was moored there, resting on a spit of shingle.

The hull was faded red, high-shouldered almost
round. The broad planked deck was beautifully-built
and balustraded, but rotten.

No cabin, just a black hole to the bilges
where the boys played a forbidden game inside her
running along the ribs to beat the rising tide.

One evening after tea, a knock
came to our door. Would we go down to help?
The boat was breaking free on the spring tide.

The whole of our end of the town was there
that night, hauling the one remaining rope
as the hull strained at the end of the harbour wall.

We held her struggling for hours
then the rope fell slack, and the old boat
turned the point and headed out to sea.

She slipped away towards the shipping lane
held in the current; a shape in the mist
broken and rudderless and alone.

The Harbour Steps

Lilias and I are sitting on the steps one evening
in the corner of the big harbour next to the boardwalk
outside the harbour master's office.
It's an industrial not a picturesque harbour.
To our left is the coal hoist and up on the right
is the massive turntable that was used
for putting locomotives on the ferry
before the railway bridge was built.
This nineteenth-century machine still works
and we used to play on it, till Eddie Gilmour crushed his foot.

We're talking about the new tan T-bar shoes
she got in Potters' in the Murraygait, and about my dress
for the school dance, a purple Dollyrocker,
and how everything in Richard Shops this year is purple, 'Why?'
and our revision: *Hamlet and Oedipus*. Was Bradley right
when he said that Gertrude just wanted
to be happy like a sheep in the sun?
We think not.
Lilias thinks Gertrude is a fantastic name,
and that from now on she'll pretend that it's her middle name
much better than Margaret, and I agree.
Lilias asks me what I think about Pat Pow.
Is she overdoing the Sandie Shaw lookalike thing?
And I say, 'The haircut is good but she should lay off the bare feet.
They're dirty and she has a verucca. I saw it in gym and it's green.'

We lower our voices, even though there's no-one there,
to mention this cream we saw in the small ads in *The Telegraph*
that you rub on your bust to make it bigger, but conclude
that although it would be dead sexy we'd never get away with it
arriving in the post. This leads us into the big question:
these brothers that we fancy. My one, I've been in love with
since the school play, and hers, she says she likes
but I'm not sure she's telling the truth.

It turns out pretty soon, surprise surprise, that wires get crossed
and we end up going out with the wrong brothers.
I go with mine for about a year and we have sex in the woods
but she is with hers, my original love interest, for ages,
and he dumps her at university and she gets an eating disorder.

Anyway, it's then that the yells and wolf whistles
start up. Some boys on bikes are circling the area
at the station next to where the level crossing used to be
till they closed the railway only a month ago.
They're opposite the Bell Rock pub and under the beige
bulk of Jubilee Buildings with that strange paved area in front;
benches that no-one sits on, and a rockery
that looks, we think, like a pets' graveyard.
Their voices carry to us clear across the harbour.

Lilias and I, who never in our lives will enter a grand box
with diamonds on our pale necks and shoulders
to a salute of raised opera glasses or a flash of lenses,
hear these anguished tenor voices aimed at us and know
instinctively how we must respond. As one
we stretch out our legs down several steps.
We're in our tightest jeans. We tilt
our pelvises and point our toes,
draw back our shoulders and stare
downwards intently from beneath our fringes.

And all the time the water in the harbour rolls
its quilting of gold light mixed with a bloom of oil;
its black reticulation of chains and mooring ropes;
its flotsam corner at the bottom of the steps, of cigarette ends
mixed with scum, its dark skirts of weed.

At the top of the steps is a square aluminium-clad bollard
where seven years later I sit to have my picture taken
wearing a nice tweed coat and brown and orange shoes.
It is the seventies by then, and I am three years married.

Broad Street Steps

I came back alone from the dance on the last train.
I'd hoped to meet friends but instead
an offshore oilman pulled me on his knee and groped
and wanted me to go to Aberdeen with him.

Then Adeline Tarbert's brother
followed me from the station into a foggy night.
'I'll see ye hame.' In Broad Street, where the steps
run between walls of whinstone starred with cresses,
he took hold of my arms and started snogging.

His tongue leapt in my mouth like a muscular fish.
I tasted his strong saliva, his cigarettes. The iron
hand rail pressed into my back, and when he grabbed my bum
and pushed against me I broke free.

'I've got to go' and he was moaning 'Naw. Mair kissin.'
I took the steps two at a time, and looked back from the top.
My jaw stung from his stubble. He was just standing
under the streetlight. His silver poplin suit
shone in a halo of mist edged with bronze.

The Haunted Town

St Andrews by the northern sea, a haunted town it is to me
  —Andrew Lang

Awareness of time arrived as sunset flamed
the broken towers at the edge of the grey North Sea.

Time haunted the wreck of the huge cathedral
and glowed in the bones of the saint.

Time carried on voices talking of their youth
in this town, the years of happiness

of drinking, dancing, lipstick, nylons, sex—
a dress of turquoise taffeta with sweetheart neckline.

So memories were laid like blazing gilded stones
across the open doorway of a mind and formed it

to pre-emptive elegy, to grieving before living
to travelling the green way of pilgrimage

while history was elsewhere, a dream
of always and never coming home.

House in the Sun

Late in the afternoon when the heat
still burns on the step at the back door
and the pointing yellow finger of light
is at its furthest reach to half way down the hall,
the dimness calls from the sitting room
a scent of flake tobacco and dusty curtains
and from behind the glass doors of the bookcase
Waverley, The Lady of the Lake and *Ivanhoe*
send out a summons. The violin
rests silent in its case on the piano.
Then the watercolours of the Scottish Highlands
grow more wavery, more pale, as the light
withdraws. Outside the open window, the white
flowers of the mock orange vibrate with bees.

Daphne mezereum *Alba*

Its flowering in February was beautiful
but every year my mother said it made her superstitious
coming at a time when people got ill
or died or there were problems with the house;
she associated the scent with sadness.

But this was not mentioned in the year
that January diagnosis was followed
by the presence in the house of bottled oxygen
my father's sudden shocking pallor, his dying
accomplished in one month.

The tiny waxen trumpets of greeny white
borne on the branching twigs of last year's wood
gave off a sharp sweet scent, filling the garden, filling
the world with loss. The mourning flowered
later as the plant put forth its dull green leaves.

White Basin

It came to the point that she was weak—
past climbing stairs and in the mornings
had to wash using the kitchen sink.

I went down Castle Street to Wallace Hughes,
Electrical and Hardware, to buy a bowl. The dark shop
smelled as always of paraffin and bare boards.

The bowl was cheap—a simple hemisphere
of thin white plastic with a rolled rim
as white and round as the full moon.

Each morning I held her upright as her white hands swam
like little fishes through the warm water. The garden
was still flowering strongly that November. I watched
her gaze at the roses through two layers of glass.

I kept the bowl and use it now for ordinary things:
handwashing and catching drips. It's as beautiful
as the moon, or as a marble basin of clear water
with fish swimming in moonlight in a dark garden.

The Map of Love

I marked the last page in the last book
you read; page two hundred and eleven
of a novel called *The Map of Love*.
I don't know if you knew it would be the last.

I kept the paper bag you smoothed over
and over with small, still-capable hands
in your last hour at home, as we
waited for the ambulance.

The bag was brown and printed
with drawings of Victorian kitchen things
jam pots and basins and jelly moulds.
You said it was a 'dear little bag'.

I helped them ease you from your bed
then from the bedroom, a second in the hall.
Out in the street, hoisted mid air
your face looked back until they closed the door.

I went straight in and stripped the bed.
Putting it in to wash, I told myself
the story that you would be coming back:
the last page in the book, the map of love.

Death

It unfolded itself within her as we watched:
a process no different from the only other time
I'd seen it, when the ginger cat died in the kitchen
stretched out in a cardboard box.

An hour before, when I arrived
she'd reared up in the bed and roared.
It was frightening, and, I believe,
her last intended conscious act, to greet me.

I said I thought she wanted
to be turned on her left side.
We settled her, head on the corner of the pillow
and held her hands.

I found myself stroking
the inside of her leg, the skin was smooth and cool.
Then, as with the cat, I felt the cold
begin to ripple up towards the heart.

Her breathing changed, and paused,
and with a sigh or two, she simply stopped.
The tide of blood ebbed fast, and beached
in a red curve on each white eyelid.

The Undertaker's Hut

The undertaker was her friend of many years:
the local joiner, who lived two doors away.
He had, surprisingly, been given permission
to build a wooden structure in his garden,
a hut, actually, for the laying out of corpses.

I remember him inviting her to take a look
and she, with a shudder, saying, 'No, thanks!
I know I'll end up there soon enough.'
So it was there, the night before the funeral
I went to see her body in its coffin.

Her corpse was hard. The hand
slightly puffy, still with its wedding band,
her face and the small neat wedge of a nose
wooden and strange. I checked
the elongated drooping mouth, the wrinkles

she had made compressing her lips,
the patch of eczema on her forehead
I had rubbed cream on just the week before.
The parts did not add up to any whole
and that was what I had prepared for

in taking my last sight. But when I stepped out
from that pleasant spartan space fragrant
with wood shavings, entering a night hard with frost,
ten steps along William Street took me
to the back door of the garden.

I stopped by the camellia, and looked
up at the blaze of stars through a black mesh
of apple boughs. It was then I shivered,
expecting her to be there, laying
a net curtain over it against the cold.

Pyre

Clearing the house I felt I had to take
the table; even though by that time
it was impossible to miss the worm holes
in the oak. It had seen so many
cups of tea and late night talks
then, ten years apart, two imminent
deaths to be discussed, hands stretched
in vain across the comfort of its grainy surface.
But all those years it stood in the same place
and it seemed cruel to move it in a van,
travelling in the dark to a strange house.
A burning ceremony seemed best;
and, at the end, all of us standing in the rain
watching the sparks fly upwards.

Chair

My mother came home pink with triumph
from the antique shop in the Seagait
next to the bus station, carrying a box
of plates, an octagonal coffee cup patterned
with wasps and cornflowers. The chair came later.

I liked its dark blue velvet and low seat
but almost immediately the chair became
my father's. It sat next to the fire beside a pile
of newspapers on a small white corner table.

Its scalloped high Victorian back
was dented by his head and always carried threads
of tobacco and strands of his silver hair.
I look at it again, look at it now
as it sits clean and empty in my hall.

Small Town Summer Evening

On the Common, there are cries from the swings,
and shouts from The Amateurs as they play
on the pitch by the caravan site
where daisies and ragged robin grow.
From there, you look across to the pavilion
that turns its back to the sea
to face the pond and the laurels
where the swans have always nested.
Once there were boats, a paddling pool
and mothers watching their children
as the boats struggled over the pond.

But the boats are gone, on this summer evening,
now, as you stand with your back to Lochend Gardens
dangerously close to the Mill Brig
where long ago your wee brother was locked in a garden shed
for eight hours, and threatened with torture by Ronnie Nelson.
Now the golden light hits the council houses, and beyond
far, far, ower the Mill Brig, tae Shanwell and Kinshaldy
the sky hangs over the dark woods and shining sands
all the way to the farther shore where the river
opens its mouth to the sea as far as Norway.
Now. You stand in this small town thinking
of lost children and their mothers,
of the coal hoist and the steam trains, and the sailors
from South America and the Baltic,
and cargoes of esparto grass and pine,
of the foundry, and the spinning mill.

Once in this town, you dreamed that at sunset
the water would rise in the harbour, and flow along Castle Street
reaching the church and the gravestones
carved with skull and crossbones, ships and anchors,
and the light would fade as the haar rolled in on the tide.

War Memorial

The last time I saw the town I'd turned
from my route on an impulse. It looked
much the same except for a rash of houses
spread on the fields to the west
where Lilias and I would walk
on summer evenings after school.

Through a crack in our old back gate
I could see that the garden was messy.
The paths were weed-grown and bald,
the roses half-strangled and desperate
but the apple tree was strong and the camellia
still there, still green.

Before I left the town, I paused by the war memorial.
Its rose beds and bowling green were peaceful
in sunshine. Bronze panels listed the names
of the dead of two World Wars, familiar
names repeated through generations in this town.
Our family name was not among them.

Lost House

Lost lost air   lost light
the rooms   the cubes   the voids
the steep geometry of stairs
the hall   where sun streamed
down from the sloping garden
through panes of violet and orange
fleurs de lis   the radiator
my father patted on his way to hospital
its battered metal the last thing touched
the thrown shadow of a cross
from window frame to bedroom floor
the ghosts of all the years
felt but ignored   their steps traversing
these boards   these passages
this intimate and detailed knowledge
the street outside   its noises
the rolling haar   the sea   the harbour
lost air   lost light